Published by Creative Education
P.O. Box 227, Mankato, Minnesota 56002
Creative Education is an imprint of The Creative Company

Design and production by Blue Design
Printed in the United States of America

Photographs by Getty Images (K.C. Alfred/San Diego Union-Tribune, Bernstein Associates, Diamond Images, Stephen Dunn, Stephen Dunn/Allsport, Focus on Sport, George Gojkovich, Jeff Gross, Tom Hauck/Allsport, Andy Hayt, Sandy Huffaker, Jed Jacobsohn, Jed Jacobsohn/Allsport, Bill Livingston/MLB Photos, Donald Miralle, Doug Pensinger/Allsport, Rich Pilling/MLB Photos, Don Smith/MLB Photos, Todd Warshaw, Todd Warshaw/Allsport), National Baseball Hall of Fame Library, Cooperstown, N.Y

Library of Congress Cataloging-in-Publication Data

Hawkes, Brian.
The story of the San Diego Padres / by Brian Hawkes.
p. cm. — (Baseball: the great American game)
Includes index.
ISBN-13: 978-1-58341-552-8
1. San Diego Padres (Baseball team)—History—Juvenile literature. I. Title. II. Series.

GV875.S33H39 2007
796.357'6409794985—dc22   2006027462

First Edition
9 8 7 6 5 4 3 2 1

Cover: Outfielder Tony Gwynn
Page 1: First baseman Fred McGriff
Page 3: Outfielder Brian Giles

THE STORY OF THE
SAN DIEGO
PADRES

by Brian Hawkes

TONY GWYNN

San Diego Padres

Victory was so close they could almost taste it. After losing the first two games of the 1984 National League Championship Series to the Chicago Cubs, the San Diego Padres improbably reeled off two wins. In the fifth and deciding game, the Padres trailed the Cubs 3–2 in the seventh inning. With two outs and a man on second base, pinch hitter Tim Flannery squirted a seemingly harmless ground ball to first. Flannery assumed he had just made out number three, but, miraculously, the ball scooted under the first baseman's glove, allowing Flannery to reach base. Soon after, right fielder Tony Gwynn hit a sharp one-hopper that took a crazy leap over Cubs second baseman Ryne Sandberg, bringing Flannery

and a second Padres runner home. Two and a half innings later, the Padres finished off the luckless Cubs 6–3, propelling San Diego to the franchise's first World Series ever.

AN ACT OF FAITH

I n 1602, Spanish explorer Sebastian Vizcaino landed his ship, the *San Diego*, at a beautiful spot along the Pacific coast just north of where Mexico and the state of California meet today. One hundred sixty-seven years later, a Franciscan monk named Junipero Serra traveled to the same location and founded the first of 21 missions that the Catholic Church would use to teach the native people in California about Christianity. Serra's mission was called the Mission San Diego de Alcalá. Soon, many other padres, or monks, came to the settlement.

One hundred ninety-nine years after Serra's arrival, a new group of "padres" established themselves in San Diego. In 1968, Major League Baseball decided to expand. The tireless campaigning of San Diego sportswriter Jack Murphy and the financial backing of businessman C. Arnholt Smith led major-league officials to select San Diego as one of four expansion sites. Like most expansion teams, the Padres were built mainly around untried youngsters and castoffs from other teams. In the 1969 expansion draft, the Padres picked up two players who would help lead the new franchise into the 1970s—center fielder Clarence "Cito" Gaston and first baseman Nate Colbert.

On April 8, 1969, the Padres made their National League (NL) debut

SAN DIEGO

Located just north of the Mexico border, San Diego is known for its beautiful beaches and sunny weather.

NO UMBRELLA NECESSARY

The city of San Diego is known for its beautiful weather and is often listed as one of the top five most visitable cities in the world for that reason. The people of San Diego take full advantage of the sunshine, spending their free time at the beach, the famous San Diego Zoo, or a host of other outside venues. If a person decides to go to a San Diego Padres game, it's a pretty good bet that the game will be played. Unless their team plays in a domed stadium, fans of other teams are often forced to bring umbrellas to the ballpark, and sometimes the games are postponed due to rain. That's rarely the case in San Diego. The Padres have been rained out only 15 times in their 35-year history. That works out to less than once every two years. Even more amazing is that the Padres went from April 20, 1983, to May 20, 1998, without a single rain-out. For more than 15 years, every single San Diego Padres home game on the schedule was played. A streak like that will probably never happen again—unless the beautiful weather of San Diego has anything to say about it.

SAN DIEGO STADIUM

against the Houston Astros at San Diego Stadium. Fans' prayers were answered as the Padres won the game 2–1. However, victories would prove hard to come by during the rest of that inaugural season. When 1969 came to a close, the squad was in last place in the NL Western Division with a dismal 52–110 record.

Despite the team's early struggles, the Padres' two new stars soon proved their worth. Gaston had a career-best season in 1970, slamming 29 home runs and batting .318, and Colbert's slick fielding and powerful swing also won San Diego fans over. He made his biggest mark on August 1, 1972, when he slugged 5 homers and drove in 13 total runs in a double-header against the Atlanta Braves. After his last home run, umpire Bruce Froemming said, "I don't believe this." Colbert replied, "Neither do I."

Although Colbert and Gaston supplied plentiful hits, the Padres had a difficult time amassing wins in the early 1970s, averaging nearly 100 losses per season between 1969 and 1973. Pitcher Steve Arlin did his best to will the team to victory, tossing seven shutouts during the 1971 and 1972 seasons. But as the losses mounted, the San Diego faithful's support was no longer constant, and rumors began to swirl that the team might relocate. Just before the 1974 season, owner C. Arnholt Smith announced that he would be mov-

PITCHER • RANDY JONES

Known for his looping curveball, Jones's method for keeping hitters off-balance worked so well that he posted back-to-back 20-win seasons in 1975 and 1976. In 1976, Jones went 22–14 with a 2.74 ERA and tied New York Giants pitcher Christy Mathewson's NL record of 68 innings without issuing a walk. Unfortunately, that year was a turning point for the worse, as he severed a nerve in his arm. Jones was never the same pitcher after that, but he didn't stray far from baseball. He now owns and operates his own barbeque stand at PETCO Park in San Diego.

STATS

Padres seasons: 1973–80

Height: 6-0

Weight: 178

- **100–123 career record**

- **Uniform number (35) retired by Padres**

- **1976 Cy Young Award winner**

- **2-time All-Star**

RANDY JONES
PITCHER

SAN DIEGO
PADRES

CATCHER · BENITO SANTIAGO

Benito Santiago entered the NL with a bang. In his first full season with the Padres, Santiago compiled a 34-game hitting streak, which set an NL record for rookies and a major-league record for catchers. Although his rookie season was his finest as an offensive player, Santiago earned a reputation as a defensive standout over the years. Blessed with an exceptional arm, Santiago often gunned down would-be base stealers from his knees. While he would contribute to other big-league teams in his career, Santiago's best seasons were with the Padres.

STATS

Padres seasons: 1986–92

Height: 6-1

Weight: 190

- **217 career HR**

- **3-time Gold Glove winner**

- **1987 NL Rookie of the Year**

- **5-time All-Star**

BENITO SANTIAGO
CATCHER

SAN DIEGO
PADRES

ing the team to Washington, D.C. It appeared as though the city of San Diego would be robbed of its team only five years after receiving it.

At the last minute, however, Ray Kroc, the McDonald's restaurant chain owner, stepped in to purchase the team, promising to keep it in San Diego. Perhaps Kroc acted prematurely, for on April 9, 1974, in the midst of an eventual 9–5 loss to the Houston Astros, a frustrated Kroc grabbed the stadium microphone and said, "I've never seen such stupid baseball playing in my life." Although he may have regretted his impulsive buy at that moment (and many others, since the season ended in the Padres' sixth consecutive last-place finish), Kroc's hard work and showmanship during the 1974 season helped the franchise draw more than one million fans to games at San Diego Stadium for the first time.

NO "NO-NO'S"

The no-hitter is one of baseball's greatest single-game accomplishments. During a no-hitter, a pitcher dominates an opposing team's batters so thoroughly that they can't muster a single hit during an entire game. As a no-hitter progresses, the fans in the stadium begin to sense that they may be witnessing history, and they usually cheer the pitcher—regardless of whether he's on the home team or not. The Padres have witnessed six no-hitters. Unfortunately, not a single one has been tossed by a San Diego pitcher. In 1970, Pittsburgh Pirates pitcher Doc Ellis fired a no-hitter against the Padres in only their second season in the major leagues. Over the years, Milt Pappas, Phil Niekro, Kent Mercker, A.J. Burnett, and Bud Smith joined an exclusive club begun by Ellis as hurlers who have thrown no-hitters against the Padres. Padres pitchers have come close on a number of occasions. Incredibly, 10 of them have carried no-hitters into the eighth inning, but all 10 allowed a hit in that inning. On the bright side, every time a San Diego Padres pitcher warms up before a game, he has the chance to become the first hurler in team history to throw a no-hitter.

PADRES

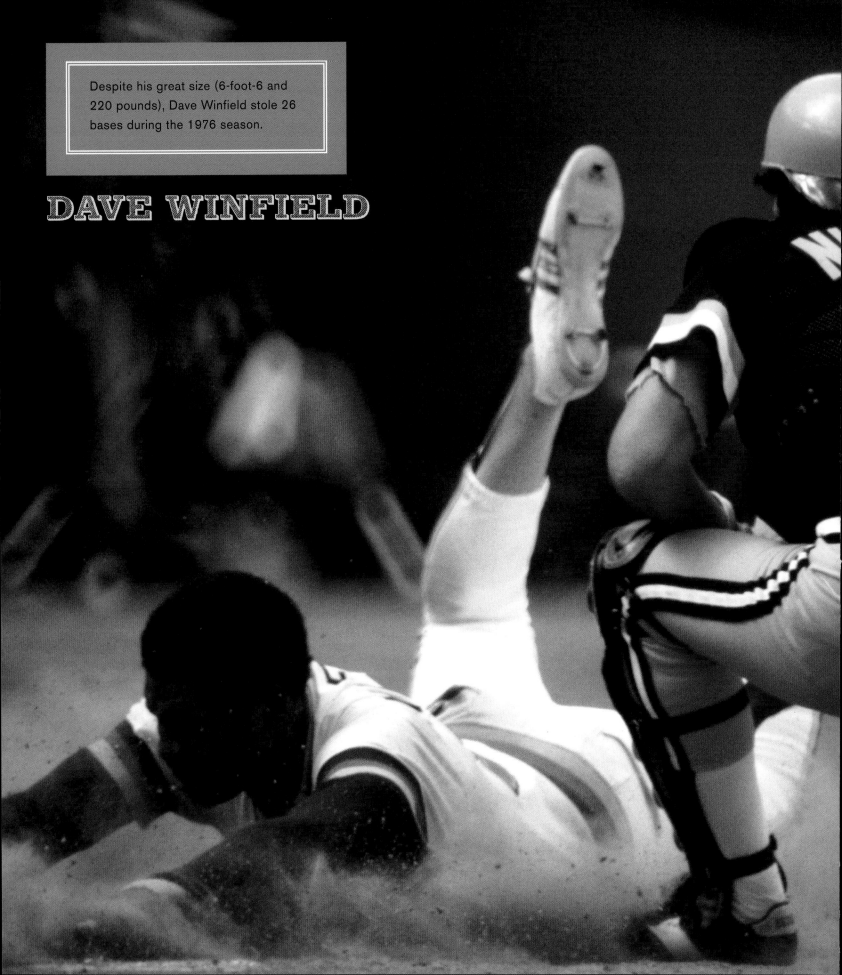

Despite his great size (6-foot-6 and 220 pounds), Dave Winfield stole 26 bases during the 1976 season.

DAVE WINFIELD

MOVING ON UP

ight fielder Dave Winfield and left-handed pitcher Randy Jones used the 1974 season as a springboard to bigger and better things, showing flashes of brilliance that would eventually pull the Padres out of the cellar. Future Hall-of-Famer Willie McCovey also lent his veteran perspective to youngsters such as Winfield. McCovey's days as an All-Star first baseman may have been behind him, but he had learned a lot about the art of hitting while with the San Francisco Giants. He took Winfield under his wing and helped shape his approach at the plate—an approach that would help Winfield achieve more than 3,000 hits in his career. Winfield took what McCovey taught him to heart, saying, "Good hitters don't just go up and swing. They always have a plan. Call it an educated deduction. You visualize."

Jones, meanwhile, became the team's first 20-game winner in 1975, using a devastating curveball that kept hitters off-balance. His pitching prowess led the Padres to 71 wins that year and 73 wins in 1976 as they slowly crept toward a .500 season and respectability.

In 1977 and 1978, Kroc brought in two more veterans to guide the team on its march toward a winning record—ace reliever Rollie Fingers and starting

GAYLORD PERRY

Gaylord Perry's pitches moved strangely, leading many opponents to accuse him of throwing illegal spitballs.

pitcher Gaylord Perry. In 1978, Fingers saved 37 games, while Perry baffled opposing hitters on his way to winning 21 games—efforts that earned him the Cy Young Award as the league's best pitcher. That same year, dazzling rookie shortstop Ozzie Smith and speedy left fielder Gene Richards added youthful exuberance to the dugout, which helped the team post its first-ever winning season at 84–78.

The Padres had high hopes for the 1979 season. Unfortunately, they couldn't duplicate the success of 1978, even with Winfield leading the team

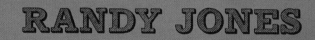

RANDY JONES

California native Randy Jones rarely struck out batters, succeeding instead by tempting them into hitting poor pitches.

THE SAN DIEGO CHICKEN

By 1974, fans of the San Diego Padres had very little to cheer about. Their Padres were a listless bunch that routinely finished in last place. It was no laughing matter—until the San Diego Chicken entered the scene. The Chicken started out at the San Diego Zoo handing out Easter eggs to children. Soon, the Chicken was making people laugh at concerts and larger events. It was only natural that the Chicken was called upon to give Padres fans something to laugh about. And laugh they did. The Chicken began appearing at all Padres home games in 1974. No matter what happened on the field, the fans knew that the San Diego Chicken would be in the stands looking for an opportunity to make them laugh. After a brief hiatus, the Chicken was brought back in June 1979 at an event called the "Grand Hatching," and 47,000 fans came to San Diego Stadium to welcome him back. Just how important was the Chicken? Years later, the San Diego Chicken was named one of the 100 most powerful people in sports by *The Sporting News*. His success and fame led to the appearance of fuzzy mascots in ballparks all across the country.

with 10 triples and 97 runs scored. His performance cemented his reputation as one of the game's best all-around players. Unfortunately, he played only one more season in San Diego before signing a free-agent deal with the New York Yankees in 1981. At the time, the 10-year, $23-million contract offered by the Yankees made Winfield the highest-paid player in the major leagues.

In the same off-season that the Padres lost Winfield, Jones was traded to the New York Mets. A year later, Smith was traded to the St. Louis Cardinals for slick-fielding shortstop Garry Templeton. Finally, Dick Williams, who had managed the Oakland Athletics in the 1970s, was hired as the new manager of the team. It was time for the new-look San Diego Padres to embark upon a new mission of winning.

DICK WILLIAMS – Managing for 22 seasons in the big leagues, Williams guided three different teams (the Red Sox, A's, and Padres) to pennants. He rarely stayed long anywhere, however, as many players tired of his strict, confrontational leadership style.

A NEW ERA BEGINS

T he 1982 season began with a whole new attitude in San Diego. As catcher Terry Kennedy described it, "Dick told us at the beginning that team play was in and excuses were out. If you produced, you played. Simple as that." The team immediately bought into Williams's message and set a new club record with an 11-game winning streak early in the season. Rookie right fielder Tony Gwynn was called up from the minor leagues on July 19, 1982, to do his part. He collected two hits in his first game—a sign of better things to come. At the end of the season, the Padres had broken even, finishing 81–81.

In the off-season, San Diego acquired veteran first baseman Steve Garvey, hoping he would provide valuable on-field leadership. Unfortunately, in July 1983, Garvey dislocated his thumb in a home-plate collision. The injury sidelined him, and the Padres missed the playoffs. Once again, the Padres' front office looked for ways to bolster their up-and-coming team, bringing in veteran third baseman Graig Nettles and hard-throwing reliever Rich "Goose" Gossage in 1984. Both Nettles and Gossage had played on championship-winning teams in the past, and Padres fans hoped their previous success would rub off on San Diego.

STEVE GARVEY

A longtime Dodgers star, Steve Garvey represented the Padres in his 10th and final All-Star Game in 1985.

FIRST BASEMAN · NATE COLBERT

As one of the original San Diego Padres, Colbert gave fans hope during the franchise's lean early years. In 1969, the young first-sacker led the team in home runs with 24. While Colbert was a consistent performer for the Padres, he didn't gain national recognition for his exploits until an August 1972 double-header against the Atlanta Braves, when he broke St. Louis Cardinals legend Stan Musial's record for RBI (11) in a double-header with his 13 runs batted in. Colbert hit home runs, drove in runners, and played a solid first base to become the Padres' first real star.

STATS

Padres seasons: 1969–74

Height: 6-2

Weight: 209

- 173 career HR

- 520 career RBI

- 3-time All-Star

- 38 HR in 1972 (2nd-most in NL)

NATE COLBERT
FIRST BASEMAN

SAN DIEGO
PADRES

Before the 1984 season began, Williams told reporters, "We've got things going for us now. We're ready." The Padres soared into first place in June, proving Williams right. Their hot start enabled them to win the NL Western Division by a 12-game margin, and they headed to the playoffs for the first time in club history. After losing the first two games of the NL Championship Series (NLCS) to the Chicago Cubs, the Padres roared back to win the series. First baseman Steve Garvey went 4-for-5 and hit the game-winning home run in Game 4, enabling the Padres to overcome a 3–0 deficit. After their decisive 6–3 win in Game 5, they were finally on their way to the World Series.

The 1984 World Series pitted the Padres against the mighty Detroit Tigers, who were led by slugging right fielder Kirk Gibson. After losing Game 1 at home, the Padres were in dire need of a victory. Into the spotlight stepped often-ignored third baseman Kurt Bevacqua, who usually watched the games from the bench. He surprised everyone by stroking three hits, including a three-run home run, to power the Padres to a 5–3 victory in Game 2. The series then shifted in Detroit's favor as the teams headed to the Motor City. There, the Tigers' bats woke up and battered the Padres' starting pitchers into submission. The Tigers went on to win the World Series in five games, but Padres fans remained proud. They had their first NL pennant.

CONSISTENTLY INCONSISTENT

I n 1985, many expected the Padres to return to the playoffs—and maybe even the World Series. Dick Williams's Padres included a franchise-record seven All-Star players, and the talented squad was a playoff contender for most of the season before falling just short of the postseason. The 1986 and 1987 seasons were disappointing by comparison. Nevertheless, rookie catcher Benito Santiago took the league by storm in 1987. He quickly established himself as an excellent defensive player, and his 34-game hitting streak set a new record for major-league rookies.

After his breakout season in 1984, when he'd collected 213 hits, outfielder Tony Gywnn had become a permanent fixture in the Padres' lineup. Gwynn's seemingly effortless left-handed stroke enabled him to line base hits to all parts of the field. A tireless worker, he studied film of both his swing and of opposing pitchers' tendencies. Armed with a bat and a plan, Gwynn became one of the toughest outs in baseball.

The Padres rebounded to post an 83–78 record in 1988. Gwynn and newly acquired second baseman Roberto Alomar led the Padres' charge in 1989, but

Benito Santiago spent his first seven seasons in San Diego, then went on to play for nine other big-league teams.

RICH GOSSAGE

HOME FIELD ADVANTAGE

When the Padres returned home on October 4, 1984, it seemed that their magical ride was coming to an end. The Chicago Cubs had won the first two games of the NLCS and seemed destined to win the pennant. In Game 3, the first-ever major-league playoff game in San Diego, starting pitcher Ed Whitson baffled the Cubs' hitters and propelled the home team to an easy 7–1 win. The Cubs rebounded in Game 4 and took a 5–3 lead into the ninth inning. Menacing Chicago closer Lee Smith needed to record just three more outs to deliver his team to the World Series, but he hadn't counted on a dramatic three-run home run by Steve Garvey, which won the game and put the Padres within striking distance of their first World Series. Game 5 would decide who was going to the World Series and who was going home. Once again, the Cubs took an early lead. The Padres staged a rally in the seventh inning that gave them a 6–3 lead. Closer Rich "Goose" Gossage took care of the rest, slamming the door on the Cubs in the last two innings and touching off a celebration in San Diego.

SECOND BASEMAN · QUILVIO VERAS

Most winning baseball teams have a spark plug—a player whose role is to get on base and jump-start his team's offense. During his three-year tenure with the San Diego Padres, Veras started many offensive rallies. Veras served as the Padres' leadoff hitter in each of his seasons in San Diego and ended his time there by leading the team in runs scored (95) in the 1999 season. Veras was also a slick fielder with a knack for taking sure base hits away from opponents with diving grabs. After the Padres traded Veras away, a slew of injuries derailed his career.

STATS

Padres seasons: 1997–99

Height: 5-9

Weight: 166

- **2-time Padres stolen base leader**

- **469 career runs scored**

- **183 career stolen bases**

- **1,554 career putouts**

QUILVIO VERAS
SECOND BASEMAN

SAN DIEGO
PADRES

even Alomar's acrobatic plays in the field weren't enough to get them into the postseason. His ability to nimbly turn double plays made him a favorite of the Padres' pitching staff, though, and often brought the San Diego fans out of their seats.

Before the 1991 season, the team orchestrated a trade that brought slugging first baseman Fred "Crime Dog" McGriff to San Diego. The following season, third baseman/outfielder Gary Sheffield came to town. For a short time, McGriff and Sheffield turned the Padres' offense into an overwhelming force that generated towering homers and a flood of runs. While the team failed to make the playoffs in 1991 and 1992, Padres fans were encouraged by the 84–78 and 82–80 finishes, and the rest of the league took notice of the slugging Padres. After one game against San Diego, Pittsburgh Pirates manager Jim Leyland muttered, "They gotta break these guys up. They just wore my pitching staff out."

The Padres struggled mightily over the next two seasons, mainly because of injuries, and in 1993, the club lost 100 games for the first time since 1974. In the strike-shortened 1994 season, the team toiled to end 47–70. Gwynn was the season's lone bright spot. He hit an amazing .394, the highest batting average in the majors since Hall-of-Famer Ted Williams hit .406 for the

ROBERTO ALOMAR – On defense, Alomar frequently turned double plays at second base, and on offense, the speedy infielder often stole second. Despite his growing stardom, the Padres traded the 22-year-old to the Toronto Blue Jays in 1990 to obtain Fred McGriff.

PADRES

THIRD BASEMAN · PHIL NEVIN

Before competing at the 1992 Olympic Games in Barcelona, Spain, Phil Nevin knew what he was going to do afterward: as the first pick of the 1992 amateur draft, he would go to the Houston Astros and begin his baseball career. In 1999, he returned to his native California in a trade to the Padres and immediately came into his own as an offensive force. Nevin led the Padres in home runs in three seasons and was named an All-Star in 2001. A fierce competitor and team leader, Nevin moved on to several other teams after leaving San Diego in 2005.

PHIL NEVIN
THIRD BASEMAN

SAN DIEGO
PADRES

STATS

Padres seasons: 1999–2005

Height: 6-2

Weight: 180

- .270 career BA

- 208 career HR

- 743 career RBI

- Career-high 41 HR (2001)

Boston Red Sox in 1941. Baseball fans throughout the country were left to forever wonder whether he could have hit the magical .400 mark if not for the strike. In the off-season, young general manager Randy Smith pulled off the largest trade in the major leagues since 1957: a 12-player deal that brought swift center fielder Steve Finley and hard-nosed third baseman Ken Caminiti to San Diego.

New manager Bruce Bochy's enthusiasm was contagious, and the 1995 team rebounded to go 70–74, a major improvement over its previous two seasons. Caminiti and Finley, as team leaders, were symbolic of the team's new attitude. They demanded that their teammates play with the same hustle they played with themselves. "Ken is just so intense," said Bochy. "It's hard to explain because I've never met anyone like him." Bochy knew that his Padres were primed for another run at the playoffs.

FRED McGRIFF – The lanky first baseman with the easy swing was the NL's home run king in 1992 with 35 round-trippers. Many Padres fans were left puzzled and disappointed when the slugger was traded away in the middle of the following season.

FRED McGRIFF

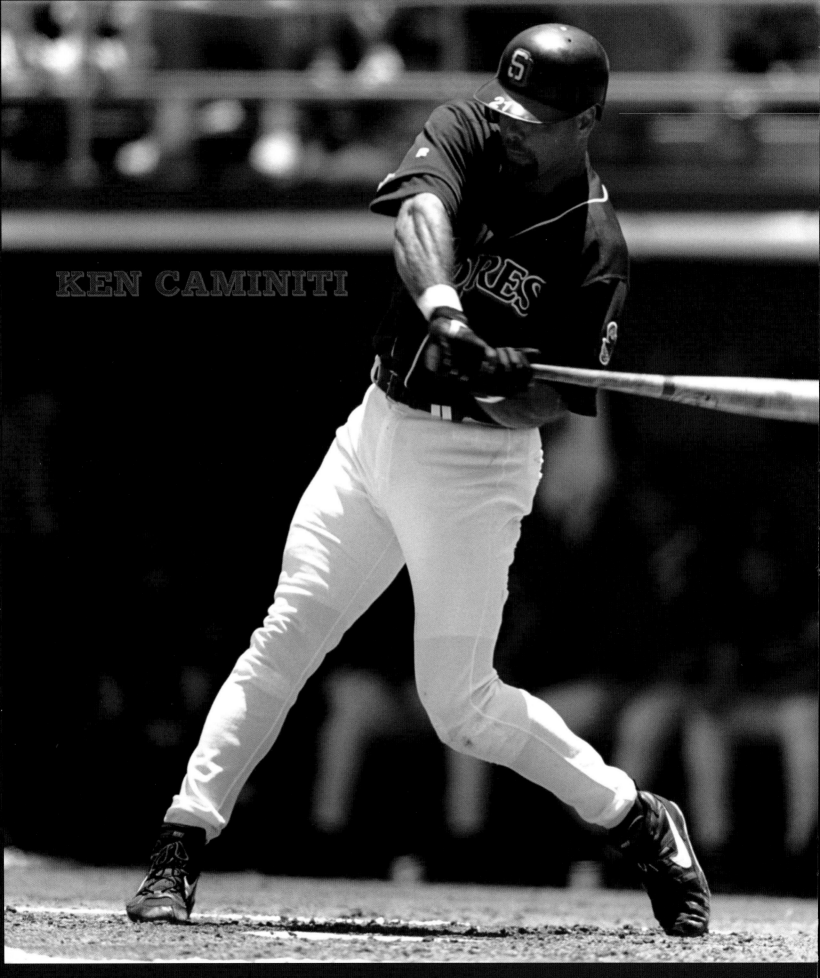

KEN CAMINITI

GLORY YEARS

The 1996 season was a memorable one for the Padres for many reasons. Catcher John Flaherty put together a 27-game hitting streak from June 21 to July 27. The Padres also made baseball history when they played the New York Mets in Monterrey, Mexico. *La Prima Serie* ("The First Series") marked the first time a regular-season major league baseball game was played outside the United States or Canada. Mexican fans came out in droves to watch the series, leading some baseball officials to wonder whether an expansion team could thrive in Mexico.

As the season wound down, the Padres and the Los Angeles Dodgers became embroiled in a battle for the NL West title. The Padres trailed the Dodgers by two games as they entered the final three games of the season, but San Diego surged to capture all three contests and win the division crown. Even though the Padres were then ousted from the playoffs by the St. Louis Cardinals, it had been a special season. Caminiti's 40 home runs and 130 runs batted in (RBI) made him the winner of the NL Most Valuable Player (MVP) award. Not to be outdone, Gwynn captured his seventh NL batting title and played in his 12th All-Star Game. Finley's fielding exploits earned him a Gold Glove, and

Ken Caminiti was famous for his toughness, often playing heroically through an assortment of injuries.

STEVE FINLEY – Finley ranked among the league leaders in extra-base hits every season, using his terrific speed to stretch singles into doubles. He eventually made it all the way home more often than not, scoring an average of 105 runs a season during his Padres career.

SHORTSTOP · GARRY TEMPLETON

After the 1981 season, the Padres traded away future Hall-of-Famer Ozzie Smith for Garry Templeton of the St. Louis Cardinals. While Templeton's career at shortstop didn't match his predecessor's in status, he was still a solid all-around player during his nine seasons with the Padres. His smooth hitting was an integral part of the 1984 season, when the Padres reached the World Series and Templeton won the Silver Slugger award as the NL's best-hitting shortstop. Since retiring in 1991, Templeton has remained in the game as a coach and minor-league manager.

GARRY TEMPLETON
SHORTSTOP

SAN DIEGO PADRES

STATS

Padres seasons: 1982–91

Height: 5-11

Weight: 190

- **329 career doubles**
- **242 career stolen bases**
- **106 career triples**
- **3-time All-Star**

LEFT FIELDER · GENE RICHARDS

Richards spent seven of his eight years in the major leagues patrolling left field for the Padres. He burst onto the scene at age 23 as the Padres' leadoff hitter and stole an incredible 56 bases. For the next six seasons, Richards remained an indispensable leadoff hitter. In 1980, Richards's best season as a professional, he hit .301, scored 91 runs, and stole 61 bases. That year, the Padres became the first big-league team to ever have three players steal more than 50 bases in one season (Richards, along with shortstop Ozzie Smith and outfielder Jerry Mumphrey).

GENE RICHARDS
LEFT FIELDER

SAN DIEGO PADRES

STATS

Padres seasons: 1977–83

Height: 6-1

Weight: 175

- **Career-high 193 hits (1980)**

- **247 career stolen bases**

- **.290 career BA**

- **2-time Padres leader in stolen bases**

Bruce Bochy's great leadership earned him NL Manager of the Year honors.

In 1998, the Padres used an eight-game winning streak in April to seize first place in the division. Second baseman and leadoff hitter Quilvio Veras helped jump-start the offense, while new ace starting pitcher Kevin Brown and closer Trevor Hoffman led the pitching staff with 18 wins and 53 saves respectively. The Padres' dominant pitching and incredible defense led to a club-record 98 wins during the regular season and put San Diego in the play-offs for the second time in three years.

In the NL Division Series (NLDS), the Padres faced off against the Houston Astros. The Padres' pitching stymied the Astros, and San Diego won the series in four tight games. Next up were the pitching-rich Atlanta Braves. Once again, the Padres' hurlers needed to be at their best. And once again, they were. Brown shut out the Braves in Game 3, and series MVP Sterling

A LATE NIGHT IN PHILADELPHIA

Double-headers have long been a part of the game of baseball. In most cases, fans are treated to two games for the price of one. With any luck, both games of a double-header can be played in six hours or less. But on July 2, 1993, in Philadelphia, the San Diego Padres and Philadelphia Phillies played a double-header into the wee hours of the morning. The first game was scheduled to begin at 4:35 P.M. However, rain delayed the start of the game by an hour and 10 minutes. Once the game started, it was delayed twice more for an additional 4 hours and 44 minutes. At 1:03 A.M., the Padres emerged with a 5–2 win, a game that not many fans in Philadelphia stayed to witness. And that was just the first game! The Padres and Phillies went on to play the second game, which started at 1:28 A.M. and went 10 innings before the Phillies were able to push the winning run across home plate for a 6–5 victory. The game ended at 4:40 A.M. and stands as the latest time a major-league game has ever ended.

Trevor Hoffman never slowed down after his great 1998 season, becoming baseball's all-time leader in saves.

Hitchcock won two games for San Diego, including the decisive Game 6. The Padres were back in the "Fall Classic."

San Diego faced off against the defending champion New York Yankees in the 1998 World Series. In Game 1 at famed Yankee Stadium, Tony Gwynn hit a home run that put the Padres ahead late in the game. However, the Yankees came back to win the game 9–6 and then swept the Padres in four straight games. Still, Gwynn put the Padres' season in perspective when he noted, "This is the most fun any of us has ever had."

CENTER FIELDER · STEVE FINLEY

Finley played for 7 teams during his 18 years in the big leagues. While with the Padres, he quickly won over fans with his Gold Glove-winning defense. He was known for getting great jumps on the ball, which enabled him to take away countless hits from opposing batters. The left-hander also had a knack for getting the big hit. Finley led the Padres in runs scored in three of his four seasons; it was no coincidence that the Padres made the playoffs twice during his stay in San Diego. The surprisingly strong Finley had two three-home-run games in 1997.

STEVE FINLEY
CENTER FIELDER

SAN DIEGO PADRES

STATS

Padres seasons: 1995–98

Height: 6-2

Weight: 180

- 5-time Gold Glove winner

- 2-time All-Star

- 303 career HR

- 1,434 career runs scored

Infielder Mark Loretta helped lead San Diego into the new century, batting .314 in 2003 and .335 in 2004.

MARK LORETTA

Hurler Jake Peavy was a rising star after leading the NL in ERA (2.27) in 2004 and strikeouts (216) in 2005.

A NEW MILLENNIUM

Before the 1999 season began, the Padres lost three key players to free agency—Brown, Caminiti, and Finley. So mainstay Tony Gwynn got his 3,000th hit on August 8, 1999, surrounded by 18 new Padres players. Hard-hitting third baseman Phil Nevin led the pack of newcomers, slamming 24 home runs, but the Padres slowly slipped down the division standings.

The Padres of 2000 and 2001 were plagued by injuries and mediocre play. In 2000, 23 players were placed on the disabled list at one time or another. Even Nevin's 31 home runs and 107 RBI weren't enough to lift the club to a winning record, and in 2001, the Padres stumbled to a 79–83 finish. That season was Gwynn's last, as he then retired from baseball. For the first time in nearly 20 years, Padres fans would be cheering on a new right fielder.

Before the 2002 season, tragedy struck when up-and-coming outfielder Mike Darr was killed in an automobile accident on the first day of spring training. While left fielder Ryan Klesko hit .300 with 29 home runs and 95 RBI, the team was unable to recover from the tragedy and finished the season in last place. The 2003 season was sub-par as well, but when the 2004 season started, the Padres looked like a much-improved squad. With an 8–2 opening day victory in their new stadium, PETCO Park, the Padres put the

KEVIN BROWN

DUELING ACES

When two aces lock horns in a pitchers' duel during the playoffs, fans are in for a treat. In Game 1 of the 1998 NLDS, Padres pitcher Kevin Brown was set to meet Houston Astros star Randy "The Big Unit" Johnson. Both pitchers were coming off stellar seasons and were looking to cement their reputations as "big game" pitchers. Brown and Johnson each held the opposing offense in check for the first five innings. Then, in the sixth, the Padres scored a run on a double by right fielder Tony Gwynn and a sacrifice fly by catcher/first baseman Jim Leyritz. The Padres added another run in the eighth inning on a home run by left fielder Greg Vaughn. In all, Brown pitched 8 innings and struck out 16 Astros, while Johnson finished the game with 9 strikeouts. The Astros were able to scratch out an unearned run in the ninth inning off closer Trevor Hoffman, but the Padres held on for a 2–1 victory and eventually won the series three games to one. Brown's incredible pitching effort in Game 1 had set the tone for a series that would belong to San Diego.

RIGHT FIELDER · TONY GWYNN

It's rare for a player to spend his entire career with the same team, but when it happens, the player often becomes the face of the franchise. Such was the case for Tony "Mr. Padre" Gwynn. He was undoubtedly one of the greatest Padres of them all—and one of the purest hitters the game has ever seen. The 15-time All-Star led the league in batting average eight times, even hitting an astounding .394 during the strike-shortened 1994 season. Gwynn's seven Silver Slugger awards (and many other honors) attest to his being one of the best-hitting right fielders of all time.

TONY GWYNN
RIGHT FIELDER

SAN DIEGO
PADRES

STATS

Padres seasons: 1982–2001

Height: 5-11

Weight: 199

- **8-time NL leader in BA**

- **.338 career BA**

- **3,141 career hits**

- **5-time Gold Glove winner**

MANAGER · BRUCE BOCHY

Bochy was with the Padres franchise for 24 seasons and was the only manager to have also played with the club. In his second season as skipper, he led the team to its first playoff series since 1984—which was also his second year as catcher for the Padres. Taking the team to two more playoffs quickly endeared him to San Diego players and fans alike. After the 1998 season, when his squad won 98 games and made it all the way to the World Series, Bochy was recognized as the NL Manager of the Year.

BRUCE BOCHY
MANAGER

SAN DIEGO
PADRES

STATS

Padres seasons as manager: 1995–2006

Height: 6-4

Weight: 210

Managerial Record: 951–975

NL Pennant: 1998

rest of the NL on notice: they were ready to rejoin the ranks of the contenders. Ace starter Jake Peavy began to reach his potential, leading the majors with an earned run average (ERA) of 2.27 and striking out 173 batters. Behind his efforts, the team compiled an 87–75 record.

The Padres' 2005 and 2006 seasons were almost mirror images of each other. The team won the NL West each year (at 82–80 and 84–78 respectively) but was then bounced from the playoffs by the powerful St. Louis Cardinals in the NLDS. The San Diego faithful were confident, though, as the Padres geared up for 2007. Peavy, Hoffman, and Chris Young anchored a superb pitching staff, and two young infielders—first baseman Adrian Gonzalez and third baseman Kevin Kouzmanoff—led a rebuilt offense. "Hopefully, it's going to be another productive year," said Hoffman before the 2007 season. "Everybody's got to pull their weight and not be content."

Since 1969, the Padres have brought pride and professionalism to the city of San Diego. Long regarded as underdogs, the Padres could always count on fine play from such stars as Tony Gwynn, but San Diego fans have faith that the new century will bring out the best in their team. With players such as Jake Peavy and Adrian Gonzalez leading the charge, the Padres have a new mission: to return to the World Series for a third time.

INDEX